TOLUCA STREET

1988

Agnes Lynch Starrett

Poetry Prize

Toluca
Street

University of Pittsburgh Press

Published by the University of Pittsburgh Press, Pittsburgh, Pa. 15260
Copyright © 1989, Maxine Scates
All rights reserved
Baker and Taylor International, London
Manufactured in the United States of America

Library of Congress Cataloging-in-Publication Data

Scates, Maxine.
  Toluca Street / Maxine Scates.
      p.   cm.
  ISBN 0-8229-3623-2. — ISBN 0-8229-5420-6 (pbk.)
  I. Title.
  PS3569.C325T65   1989
  811'.54—dc20   89-4859
                                                         CIP

I would like to thank the editors of the publications in which these poems, sometimes in earlier versions, first appeared: *American Poetry Review* ("A Boat," "1956," "The Orchard," and "We Never Knew You"); *Antioch Review* ("Wartime"); *Calapooya Collage* ("Smoke"); *Crazy Horse* ("Hospital"); *5 AM* ("The Border"); *Hubbub* ("Reading Grimm's Fairy Tales"); *Ironwood* ("A Journey," "Let Go," and "Vision"); *Massachusetts Review* ("Desire in America" and "Floor Plans"); *Missouri Review* ("Salem: Two Windows"); *Northwest Review* ("The Garden"); *Poetry East* ("Birthday," "The Drunkard: Our Song," and "Night Sounds"); *Prairie Schooner* ("The Weavers" and "Working"); *Quarterly West* ("A Ferry Crossing"); *The Raddle Moon* ("For June"); and *The Seattle Review* ("Cathedral").

I wish to thank the MacDowell Colony for a fellowship which assisted me in writing and revising many of these poems.

I also wish to express my particular gratitude to Maggie Anderson, Bill Cadbury, Deb Casey, Brigit Kelly, Michele Piso, and the late Ann Stanford for their generous support and encouragement through the years.

In the poem "The Teacher," the italicized line, *"It has been falling for weeks now"* is from Ann Stanford's poem "By the Woods, Reading," from her book *The Descent.* This same line also appears as the epigraph for "Smoke." In the fifth stanza of "The Teacher," the italicized line, *"Where is the white horse"* is from Ann Stanford's poem "The White Horse," from her book *The Weathercock.* In the last stanza of "The Teacher," the italicized line, *"I will remember you into light"* is from Ann Stanford's poem "Memorial," from her book *The Descent.*

*The publication of this book is supported by grants
from the National Endowment for the Arts
in Washington, D.C., a Federal agency,
and the Pennsylvania Council on the Arts.*

Contents

Contents

A Journey

THE TEACHER

The Teacher

to the memory of Ann Stanford

On the day I learned of your death
my friends asked me to read to them.
It was raining,
midsummer in a farmhouse.
I read one poem
the poem that begins with a line from one of yours
It has been falling for weeks now
and I didn't tell them. I couldn't tell them
what I'd known all day.

This was the first year
I could have told you what it was like at twenty,
could have seen, do see
how every morning
I sat on the stone bench
by the mock orange trees
waiting for you to walk by on your way to class.
I'm on that bench waiting.
I've been waiting for years.
I'm at the arena ushering roller derby.
I'm selling tickets at the Queen Mary.
I'm shoulder-to-shoulder in the hallways after Cambodia.
I'm watching the helicopters overhead
because Reagan has shut down
every state college in California.

I understand nothing.
I've barely made it this far.
But every morning I sit on the stone bench
because it is all I have
because I'm in love
waiting for you, a woman, a poet, to pass:
I've found you and I've read all your books.
I've read the poems until they are in me.
I take the lines

and scatter them around the woman
who stands in front of the class
because I want to see how each word falls into a life.
And that begins it,
that begins the life of the word.
If I read now what I wrote then
I can remember every word you said.
I can remember sitting there head down
saying nothing,
until finally I read a poem out to the class
and you said: "There, there
you've done it."

Later that evening
when I did tell my friends, they asked
"What was it?"
"How did she touch you?"
And I answered that after awhile
you said: "I can't teach you anymore *now*."
And when you said *now*
I knew you believed I could learn more.

I didn't tell them about the first night
I came to your house,
winding my way up the canyon
arriving early before the others.
I sat outside in my car
watching you move in the kitchen,
a woman ordinary enough there in that circle of light.
I was afraid.
I wanted so much. I didn't know
what you could see in me
but I wanted to see it in you. Years later
you told me you knew I was out there.
And later that night,
for the first time up all night writing,

4

I began to know there was something outside my life
that my life would go on day by day
but there would be something else.
It was there
in the wind, in the walnuts, in that canyon.
I remembered the white horse.
I remembered the line
Where is the white horse?
I remembered the towhees drowning in the trough
as if I were there on that hillside with you
in the wind—that wind—
so then I knew eucalyptus,
I knew it swinging over the road on the way
to the state hospital to visit my grandmother
on Sundays, the cars pulled to the side,
the passengers stealing tomatoes from the fields.
I'd had no memory,
I didn't know where I came from
and now you were listening
and though all I could see then was loss
now I knew there was a story.

But I did tell them that it was years
before I understood
that I was beginning to learn the rest of what
I had to learn,
before I understood that what you had seen in me
didn't belong to me at all.
That was your gift to me—
there—that was the place
where my life bent away from itself
to join something else,
just as when we say
it did not happen to only me
we begin to give up the self,

saying it happens to all of us
and that is when we begin to hear
and to speak and to give up our silence.

✻

Earlier that evening
when I had said nothing
I looked out at the rain
thinking of another time
when after a long journey
I had come home changed
to a pouring rain in midsummer—
as I stood on the porch
one of the Bach cello suites,
that exquisite music
the bow of the cellist
laboring, occasionally scraping the strings,
played behind the curtain of rain
until music and rain flowed together—
and then, on that evening,
I thought, I am remembering you,
I will remember you into light
the dense rain,
the others moving in the kitchen behind me,
and the green field on an evening in July
where through the window I saw the chair
the child had dragged out earlier in the day
to sit and read under the only tree,
a huge oak that drew the field around it.

ANGEL'S FLIGHT

Angel's Flight

Memory is as narrow
as the porch where I sit next to my brother
over twenty years ago,
as the street my mother is crossing
with my grandmother to visit a neighbor,
as the track of the trolley
we rode that morning
in the city of angels.
My brother ten years older
and remembering it
when, on our way here,
to my grandparents' house,
my mother urged him to stop the car
so we could ride Angel's Flight
one last time. And so we rode
for a nickel, a rickety trolley
up a steep hillside no one lived on anymore.

And now we sit on the steps
watching my grandfather make his way
up Toluca Street,
the city below us layered in yellow haze.
Everything that is important to me is here,
everything I loved first:
the old man, my brother,
my mother leading her silent mother
across the street she will not cross alone,
and this dusty porch
and sagging house with all of its history,
the photographs on table and piano top
and the sunroom in front
piled with newspapers.
Because as a child, I loved
what had happened before me—
my father
rising through the unnatural light of the city
as he walked up this hill from the war,

my mother and small brother
waiting on this porch for him to return—
as a child loves looking back
because she cannot imagine the future.

I didn't know then
the history of my grandmother,
institutionalized at thirty-two
after giving birth to her seventh child
in fourteen years, of the years after that
when the old man
wouldn't let her come back to the house,
of the bigotry bred
so deeply into our family
that my grandmother,
the daughter of Lila Dolores Orozco,
was lost to us.

That old man,
the awful glow of the city,
and my father's awaited deliverance
on a bus from Long Beach
into a life that still wouldn't work,
were what I knew to love
because my mother had passed me
the best of her memories
letting me imagine this street,
deserted now too,
as a passage into another time
happier than the life we were living then,
and just as in her eyes
a rickety trolley became a dying angel
as it climbed a battered hillside
with no longer any place to go,
all of them seemed blessed for a moment
in some other light.

1939, Day and Night

Only diapered, talcumed
in the worst heat wave in years.
He's too small to do anything
but wriggle, mewl his complaints
from the bassinet.

The landlord sleeps in his bathtub,
not in it, on it, laying boards
along the rim. He never bathes.
This afternoon he sits on the splintered
stairs eating melon, slicing
as he goes. The sidewalk is littered
with hunks of shrinking rind.

Housing is hard to come by. Your son
can grow right into the fingerprints
some other child smeared beside
the window frame. No, you'll
scrub them off. Small boys
squat in the alley flipping pocket knives
in mumblety-peg. Pigeons angle
toward the shadows of the bridge.

Emerald Street. The bare mound
of the hill butts the stucco
of your building. Your breasts
so full you stuff your blouse
with diapers to sop the milk.
One night there was what your husband
called *horseplay* in the rooms below.
Someone fired a gun. The bullet
whizzed up through the floor, right
past the baby's head.

Wartime

I thought I heard him speak of it,
and if my father had killed a man
that would be part of the answer.
This death would be different
from those in the war
that he cried over Saturday night
while the TV played back old newsreels
and he sat with his scaling feet up
suffering from jungle rot.

Then he'd never made it to shore.
A plane, a face he hadn't seen,
sliced his ship in half leaving him
and others in the water for days.
He'd joke his webbed feet kept him alive
and I'd look at the spot on his arm
where he'd had a tattoo scraped away,
think of it as the blurred wound left
to a man who had almost drowned,
seeing him fade into the scar only
to be rescued just in time.

The real killing came only once.
Mother whispered it was an accident.
It happened while hauling lumber
through the redwoods
where he and his truck are at home:

The war is over, the man who stands
by the side of the road isn't even a question.
And you think he's met your glance,
your hand raised in greeting,
your thoughts already rolling on
past your hand coming down to rest
on the wheel again, when he steps
in front of your truck
having never seen your face.

Working

All those women working,
laughing on their lunch break.
You found work the day after high school,
stopped for the first child
until war called you. Jarred
by a punch press, your own wounds were
bandaged hands resting on your knees.
Now there was something
just beyond your touch.

Standing in front of the police bulletin
pencil poised, pad in hand:
Back at work, I got pregnant with you.
The neighbors lean over chain link fences
where nothing's growing yet.
Wide open, at night the air smells
of ghost beanfields. The dairy calendar
reminds you of what mothers should know:
milk is important, recipes
for holding your man, notes to yourself
to call the dentist, record my first words,
feed the roses.

Thirty years later this gift,
a tablecloth that never touched your table:
you crocheted the same pattern
every night until I was old enough
for you to go back to work
and centerpieces for your mother,
sisters, every sister-in-law.
The stitches change from beginning to end.
It took so long and you were changing.

His dinner wasn't served,
notes for turning on the oven
and bringing in the clothes.
You had deserted.

I halfway believed him:
no milk and cookies, no aproned mother
bending over me. You paid for the only
vacation we ever had. You wore a bathing suit.
Intruders, my brother and I
found you sleeping in a clearing—
that blue dream of a lake.

Floor Plans

It was $8,000 with a GI loan
and thirty years to pay it off,
numbered streets to the south,
over to Hindry for catechism.

The house across the street
where the bachelor died, the same record
repeating for days like an echo
of his last cry, is Debbie Kimmel's
where a union picket, cornered
in an unfamiliar maze, was shot
beneath her bedroom window. And
Carol Jenson's past the front door
to her mother's bedclothes bunched
on the sofa.

North across Aviation to junior high,
Carol and Debbie wave or signal
something's wrong, that somnambulist
fumbling with his crotch walks
past me. Funny, until the afternoon
I'm alone. Then I run.

Two Kathys live in duplexes
at opposite ends of the tract.
One father riffling through train magazines;
the other a trail of grease on an armchair,
gone to the small hotels
where fathers stay downtown.
There, on a window of my grandparents' house
five stars for sons and sons-in-law
are still stuck to the pane.
Inside, a room smells of no one
having slept in it for years.
The bed pulls out from a bureau drawer,

like a relic bleeding on its saint's day,
it unwrinkles into place.

And beyond that house my cousins live:
four families, two in the same model,
Schwinns tangling in the driveway.
Their fathers, like mine,
march off to Water and Power every day.

Angel

This child is an angel . . .
The priest drank at her wake,
cassock swaying like big leaves falling in rain,
as he washed down
and was not meant for this world.

And what did she love but photos of the dead,
or the ebb of our grandfather's strength
as he grew close to a natural death?
Her parents could not bear this,
and she saw, as the adults gathered
on Sundays after church
that they did not want her,
that they all believed
she was the little offering,
the one in every generation who had seen
the other side.

Queen of Angels. Hospital
in a city ironic with names, nuns
still wearing habits then, trailing
the halls like her sisters' voices trail now
as they ask *What happened?*

What visible sign besides at seven
what she did to her body
that willed its release,
the call to dinner falling over our heads
in the corner of the yard,
one child saying to the other,
I don't eat.

Some make it through the little deaths,
but she had seen enough
and did not long for this world,
her bones sinking in that knowledge that knew,
that knew, and asked for nothing.

Dancing and Dinner

I came in the back door
and in the living room
was Johnny,
whose name I'd only heard,
and his wife and his two boys
and something frantic.
They were dancing.
Johnny swinging one arm
around my mother's waist
and swinging back to his wife.
No music
but it was contagious
the boys and I suddenly not shy,
wheeling each other around the room.

We went out to dinner.
We were dreaming. The children
bent over Shirley Temples,
those fake drinks,
the ashtrays and shot glasses
just out of that rim of light.
And then the adults were silent,
we children sleeping in the back seat
all the way home.

Weeks later, my father and I
were eating Chinese food up on Manchester.
We were sitting by the window,
my father drinking beer after beer
until he looked up at the owner
limping out of the room and said:
"You know Mike has no meat in his leg.
He lost it in the war.
And Johnny's dead. He shot himself."

And then I knew
how Johnny's boys ran,
how they twisted and crouched
as if their own backyard were a minefield
until they finally fell
holding each other
in the dust under the orange trees
after seeing their father's blood
on the living room floor.

For June

The moment of change is the only poem.—Adrienne Rich

It was a game
they played that afternoon,
Saturday, nothing else to do,
two drunks on a lawn swing
gliding under a skinny peach tree
talking about each other's wives:
"Bitch, bitch," they nodded.
I sat between them, and the wives?
Both knew enough to stay away
from this and each other.
They were in their kitchens, fuchsias
waving from the windowsills.

June, after all these years
mother writes that you're afraid to go
out of the house again,
though this time it's death
haunting you.
Then, I loved your cool house,
shuttered on weekday afternoons while you
were the other mother, your tears,
a malady I clung to, an illness
mother described as *up and down.*
Then, you were the one
they could make cry.

As if they had planned it,
my father blocked our doorway
when you ran toward it:
"Don't come over here with your troubles."
You froze in the driveway,
outside, and the world only as big
as the strip of concrete between two houses.

20

Before mother reached him
you'd started back. In the moment
neither of you could change,
he stood between you,
shouting, "Go home, bitch, stay away
from my house."

1956

In Nick Ray's "Bigger Than Life"
a poor schoolteacher's life is saved
by the miracle drug cortisone,
but still untested it gives him
delusions of grandeur: he buys
his wife expensive clothes
she won't ever wear in their
small house, hurls a football
at his chubby son for hours on end.
Finally he wants, like Abraham,
to sacrifice the boy for the sake
of discipline. He wakes
in a hospital bed. The diagnosis:
he took too much and wanted more.

A dose of too much hope, then
things got out of hand, or something
catches up with you. On weekends
father plants the perfect rose garden.
In a rainstorm he joins the neighbor men,
straining like the famous photograph
of raising the flag on Iwo Jima,
they push a Chinese elm
against the wind.

One afternoon he rescues
his old treasure, the Bataan knife,
and seeing no flag of surrender
tries to corner mother
between counter and sink.
The police leave him alone,
part of the conspiracy his family
can't understand. Now gifts:
the blue velvet rhinestone bathrobe,
the genuine handtooled leather purse.
But it's too late, nothing saves him.

As a child I stood next to my father
watching a lumberyard fire
and caught Eisenhower's eyes
on a campaign billboard hovering
above the flames. Nick Ray asks the question
of what it was—them, or something
in each of us waiting to go wild?
We were the little people,
those were our lives.

Birthday

On the West Coast
it's five in the morning,
but my mother,
dreaming she speaks to me,
has awakened herself
and through the phone lines
continues here
where I am eating breakfast
surprised she speaks to me,
because it's there, in dreams,
where my father walks from room to room
saying *I am sorry, sorry*
that I can barely hear her.

In dreams
she's stitching buttons after work
on my angry brother's coat
torn from the clothesline by my young dog.
She's standing at the kitchen sink
cleaning fish one by one
from a gray bucket
a neighbor has brought in out of the fog.
When I stare at their dead eyes
she says
You don't have to look.
She wishes she didn't either,
the hem of her dress grazes the rim
of the bucket,
their eyes seeping something cold
into our kitchen light.

In dreams
I stand at her bedroom door
having gone into the house
one last time to say good-bye.
And it's because I can't stay there in the life

she's finally made for both of us
that I whisper *Mother,*
leaving is the best thing I can do.
Though all she'll say,
still in bed and half asleep
is *I know, I know.*

And now I know
my mother's loneliness was so large,
that, like the fog that banked the streets
when she walked home at night,
it couldn't be seen or heard.
And there in dream
that long dead dog still beats
its hungry path.

Night Sounds

In summer you heard what you heard:
father and son rolling out the front door
into the yard,
a fist through the windshield
as the boy pulled away from the curb
swearing not to come back,
his father screaming what would happen
when he did.

Here, night has its own volume:
one evening arguing
from one end of the house to the other
we spilled out to the stairs
until a tree falling silenced us,
its weight scraping and bruising other trees
as it fell, the earth beneath it
finally shifting and settling.

I think of this now
having crossed the tree in the woods yesterday,
of the old buck
my friend says he sees rooting alone
under the moon in the neighbor's garden,
of a day weeks ago
when, in a moment between what you wanted
and I wasn't able to give,
you wouldn't let go of me, until I cried out—
frightened by what it meant
to hold on so tightly.

I can hear their fists
making their sweep through the air
somebody landing a blow,

ending each time
in the closest they'd come to any embrace:
my father's body falling
then pinned to the carpet,
my brother rising now
ready to make his leap for the door.

Ice

When we arrived
my friend walked ahead of me,
down a street but out of place
among the rows of mustard housing.
Too hot to move;
the men were in the rec room
watching the Pirates and the Giants.
That night
the family next door,
visitors as well,
cracked peanut shells for hours.

At breakfast my father
told me again the story of buying our house.
He saw my mother wanted it
because she cried when he'd never
seen her cry.
He stopped the car
and still sees that turning,
the gravel spitting
on the as yet unpaved road.

For years he did what he had to
and then he stopped. Something
wiped routine away.
And now in a wheelchair
for no reason
I can see, he's too weak
to take it on the street. I said
they'd fix everything in time.
He said it was too late.

At dusk the car seemed part
of the flat landscape,
still light enough
to see our progress

past stalled farm equipment,
the twisted rows of olives.
Until the sky reddened then blurred in darkness,
the way sadness can take over
when anger loses focus.

We'd driven all day,
the motel room was too hot.
My friend said it hurt to touch
her eyes, her cheeks, even her hair,
surprised at how the body
seemed to give out.
It was easy to say
it's then we take care of each other,
to bring her ice.

Perfume

I know the perfume
of a woman who held me as a child.
Tonight it blurs my hands,
the cloth of my blouse.

On occasion
she wore silk, pearls
trailing into a world
other than our blank street.
She was lonely on hot afternoons
lifting her fingers through my hair,
my head pillowed against
her generous flesh.

She's dead. And dying
waited to outlive what had gone wrong
her body breaking down,
air pressing in
the way wind tears clouds apart
flaying them like a whip to tissue.

I wrote to tell her
that I was seven, crying
the day their Buick pulled away
to a new neighborhood, to ask
if she remembered the red clown,
the cardboard squares of her son's
circus ring. I didn't say
I remembered her touch.
I'd return it now, hold her
through that scent of soap, camphor
clinging from the trees out in the yard.

We are temporal,
our bodies the sum of all we'll know.
But something happens

outside of ourselves.
That fragrance,
the layerings of air
I sank closer to her through,
yields now
like the door to her familiar house.

Smoke

It has been falling for weeks now.—Ann Stanford

By now the roads out in the country
are familiar, each will lead
back to the other. The produce stands
are closing up, nothing left but apples
and winter squash, pumpkins
if we'd carve them.

The pumpkins are luminous
drifting in fields of yellow fog,
the whole scene almost beautiful
though it's stagnant air
smoke from our chimneys cupped over the valley.

Every fall farmers burn their grass fields.
When the wind shifts suddenly,
smoke pours into the city. It happened
last month, isolating the sun like a fireball.
The day turned sulfurous
reminding me of a photograph
of elderly relatives on an anniversary:
tinted gold to enhance their occasion,
it gathered too the uncle who stood by their side
heightening the olive drab of his uniform
and his auburn hair.

That sky and trees were gold as well
would not have been unusual. Every fall
of childhood was a season of fires.
For weeks I've remembered one day in October:
the windows open, *santana*
blowing. Across the alley a woman
reels in laundry shaking off cinders
before folding each shirt into a basket.
Now the blocky bodies of my aunts
move through the room, their shoulders
lambent in the smoky depths of afternoon.

Easter, 1984

I spent last night halfway to heaven
on a rooftop gothic with crosses.
Below me,
just when I thought I wouldn't see them again,
my mother and her sisters
were trudging uphill,
and for a moment I thought
them still stunned by my grandmother's
long scream against words
those deadly hours of sensible talk,
until I saw it was practicality,
one foot in front of the other,
saving each of them.

Toward morning,
buoyed through the night on their shoulders,
I found myself watching the planes
lower themselves through the smog of a city,
and then I knew that dirty cushion
was all the dead souls
that soften our falling.
Finally, I woke to lilacs,
the new screen of green leaves,
still thinking of my grandmother,
the Easter she came back into the present
to cook, to make divinity,
her daughters sighing over that sacred act
in a house where there was no room
for the presence of what anyone
could call divine.

And we sighed today
standing in the kitchen drinking and chopping,
women in our thirties
wondering where we'd be next year,
old enough each of us to have been our own mother,
twisting the spoon through the soup
singing to the child on the hip.

The Lifting

i.

We were arguing about influence
drinking too much
and burning green wood in a cabin on the coast,
until the room filled with smoke
the air hanging between us
as if filled with our own ghosts.

The next morning
we stood on a cliff
looking out at an ocean
gray with churning
watching for the brown skin of sea lions
or flash of black seals
but we finally saw that the whole sea was alive,
prehistoric with spouting.
The gray whales were migrating,
some of them so close to the shore
we could see the long arch of their spines
mottled with barnacles.

ii.

There's no sun here
so I'm back in November
buying straw flowers and eucalyptus
in the Mission, flower stores
on every corner and later the blue glare
of the bay from the hills in Berkeley.
Standing in a friend's kitchen
we're talking all night into morning:
the old question of whether to go on,
what to go on to.
Out the window
clotheslines cross the courtyard

and the small gardens below
turn to compost.

I understand
this bare high-ceilinged kitchen,
the sighting of neighbors on their landings,
wooden steps with shaky railing
dropping two stories down to the gardens.
In a garden like these my mother's stories
leave chickens flapping and headless,
their necks wrung on the clothesline,
among flower pots filled with cactus
among the birds her grandmother raised
singing in their own oasis
in that dusty garden
in the middle of Los Angeles
twenty-five, fifty, or eighty years ago
on a street filled with its sturdy relief
of sound and movement
and family
of which I am forever a part.

iii.

I'm learning to be alone,
watching what flutters
out of the corner of my eye:
a bird, brown wren,
blows off the woodpile into the snow,
the dark edges of the eucalyptus
turn papery, framed
in this afternoon light.

I miss the sea
sixty miles away, the big fishing boats

drawing into the bay at Newport,
curve of the WPA bridge at Waldport
tide pulling out,
where we walked years ago
on the wet beach without rocks or shells
just the tracing of seaweed.

iv.

So much is unrealized,
the distances between all of us
are filled with the bodies of memory,
our past where nothing changes
except for the way it comes into the present,
and here everything happens again and again.
On a street corner at dusk
it's not that I am still a child
but what I've remembered and why
that has become this moment as well:
lifting a bird from the gutter,
I've chosen to remember the lifting,
though I chose not to remember the weeks afterward
wings mending in its cage in the corner of the garage,
I remember the sky opening,
bleeding bird in my hands,
the lifting.

THE BORDER

Cathedral

The midsummer sky
is closing over us,
the cathedral in the distance.

In this light, it's as if the rosy stone
could breathe, softened by gentian,
hollyhock, roses climbing everywhere.
A cat dozing on a garden wall or a dog
guarding a rooftop hint at private lives
in the courtyards below,
otherwise terraces, pub signs,
a cityscape of smaller spires
are cast against its every angle.

Along the narrow streets
the newspapers shout
a lord's son has done himself in.
If so, his name won't go on the cloister wall,
but inside the regimental chapel lists
the hundred campaigns,
all the families with one son.
Out past the plane trees
everything is preserved, including
the bishop's first bell-ringing swan.

In the graveyard
they're excavating the several layers
reburying the dead as they go:
the sixteenth century male,
hands folded, gapes at the sky.

We're like him
or the peasants who dropped
their ploughed-up Roman spoons
by the roadside as they entered town.
Nothing for our eyes but the tower
and the gargoyles, weathered, happy,
necks craning against the sky.

The Weavers

The domes of haystacks
are covered by white cloth, orange
stubble stretches beyond them, fuchsias
grow in hedgerows like sprung stars: these
are the brightest colors in a land with little sun
and few trees. In the archways
of castles and abbeys the faint green and pink stone
is the underside of centuries of mist. Toward
the horizon a field of heather
slips into the watery distance.

At Drombeg Circle
the ashes of a child
were found under the center stone
and the earth tamped down
where they must have danced. A farm woman,
her red madonnas tucked into alcoves
and a voice like haze,
whispers that when a French oil tanker went down
sixty men died and one woman,
the baker's wife,
who must have known something
because when they found her
she still wore her handbag over her shoulder.

Uneven fences of stone
climb and cross hillsides. These plots,
some flecked with sheep,
grow smaller and smaller, falling
like a mosaic into the next valley.
Now I remember the Sullivans
and their seed potatoes and their reasons
for leaving the Roaring Water for America
for the coal pit Dennis Sullivan fell into
where he was blinded,

and I remember one daughter
named Lucy which somewhere meant light.

At dusk a flock of small birds
flies in formation, each time they shift
one bird holds the circle until the new circle forms,
again and again over our heads
one bird holds the circle.

Nightfall

At dusk the nun
leaned her forehead against the train window
and whispered *addìo, addìo,*
a small cry not to God
but of farewell
to her sister standing
on the platform,
for a moment isolated
outside the flat symmetry
of night or day.

Tonight
the child was dressed for church
because it was a holy day.
She stood on the sidewalk
staring at the priest
at the top of the steps. And
what I saw was light from the interior
folding over his robes, and the hitchhiker,
a sailor my father stopped to pick up,
his eyes illuminated for an instant
like an animal caught
by the side of the road
that waits to make a crossing
on into its life.

I saw the child
in the crossing, something
she might later call anticipation
as day went on long after night had fallen,
and the sailor's eyes,
their translucence,
what I couldn't yet begin to call
mortality. Until he bent,
stamping out his cigarette,

into the car
breaking its placid atmosphere
and sealing it again
as he joined us
head resting on the dark.

Yesterday
I found a bouquet of wildflowers
cradled under the spout of a fountain
and remembered how sometimes,
like the simple shafts of allegory
straight from God,
I've told myself
one word unlocks the soul.

A Boat

Each evening at sunset
one boat sits in the harbor.
Lit prow to stern
it's like childhood,
a peripheral memory. The boats
they call *tenders* ring around it,
and the masses of low islands
recede in the dark.

We've finished talking.
Beyond the olive trees where
the birds sleep, its mast,
certain as our differences,
bisects the stars. On board
the fishermen sift fingerlings
from the nets as they let them run
through their hands
for signs of a tear.
Their big dog
who rides to sea with them each day
is pacing the deck.

At dawn the night boats come home.
The birds, large and small,
sweep uphill in one wave of sound
before they divide for the day.
I've dreamt of a woman
who dreams her own death.
It began with her heart.

The men walk uphill with so little,
some red mullet in a plastic bag.
They've cast their lights
down through the green sea
seen the wide tunnel of fish;
they can't catch them.

Crete

I was reading Homer,
things happened
and there was every reason as to why—
the gods appeared in each dream,
in the form of bird or friend,
to lift fishhook, vase,
and bowl of dailiness.

One morning
when I saw a woman leading a donkey
up the far hillside
carrying buckets of the night's refuse,
I saw that hours earlier I'd dreamt
a blow to my head, a terrible slamming,
something crushing—
and then I was alone:
my coat my only house,
I cut a swath through a deep green sea
I knew was death. And at that window
I let myself believe that woman led my dream
of the future away.

But held in the world of dream, of ocean,
sky, and olive grove—
no border between the body and the soul
climbing the stars each night—
whatever moments we construct to tell our story
had just begun to fall away.
And what I saw then
was not my future, but my past,
where I had come close to death already,
where long ago
someone had let me go,
let me go wildly into the world much too soon.

Our lives are not ordered
but barely sensible,

and when these moments speak to us
we do not want them
we will not hear them—though
they are what we have always known—
those small birds twittering
against a wall
made of nothing
but what we are trying to forget
because we wish it were not so.

To a Friend Who Has Lived Here

It is December
luna means moon, and *cuore*
the heart, from the headline
il cuore plastica.
You want to know
the names of the streets
I am walking. You want to know
what it is I see.
In all the years you said *Italy*
I never saw loneliness
breaking into its own language.

This morning
in the candlelit tomb of a church,
looking at a crucifix
that had survived through the ages
the chest wound,
the wound each artist repeated
until it blossomed even in shadows,
was quiet.

Then I heard my mother
murmuring her confession to the priest
on Saturday, remembered
my grandmother on the only night
I ever spent with her, how
she knelt by the bed she slept in alone,
the crucifix bleeding into the blue wall
above her head. Until finally
I saw someone I love, you,
turning away from me and the fear
that kept me from following.

I walk by the river,
il fiume, its mist rising in plumes.
I hear myself speaking the other language,

its few words are the bridge
I've crossed into it by.
And inside loneliness,
con una spina nel cuore,
this sickness of the heart,
I see so much of our lives
are spent in its hollow space
between wanting and asking.

The Orchard

From the top of this hill
the walled orchard slopes
down the hillside
and unpeopled roads
wind through it.
It is the hour
of walking home from school,
the dead intimate hour of childhood
when my parents had not yet
come home from work.
The trees
they planted were a promise
that outlasted them,
a length of slender trunk
and a rootball hauled home
in a gunnysack
that in three or four years
would lean heavy with fruit.

In this air
yellow as old newspaper,
I'm walking up Toluca Street
to my grandparents' house,
the oil well churning
behind the gritty fence on the hilltop,
the roots of the plum trees
twisting up through the sidewalk,
my family's bitter words
breaking over my head
like a dissonant note
drifting up from the city below me
where one bell is ringing off-key,
ringing over my life.

All autumn
we have said what we have to,

all anyone can. The sun has set
behind one stone wall.
It is already dark
in the city,
in the corridors of the museums
and the interiors of churches
coated with incense and age.
An old man passes me now.
He won't smile,
his gun tucked under his arm;
the boy is behind him,
the rabbits slung over his shoulder,
their coats slick
with the rain, with their own blood.

In the orchard
the branches are raking the sky
and the careful pruning of one tree
next to another
butting its thick trunk
through the dull planking of a shed
is something I already knew.

Going to Mass After Fifteen Years

Just off his motorbike
the boy rushed through his part
of the epistle.
His jeans and sweatshirt
already part of the life
in front of him,
the Latin he mumbled
like the language of childhood,
like the altar boys shifting
behind him on the steps of the altar,
like the months I've spent
away from home
where what had been present
and the past
all seem part of another life.

I knelt
I wanted to remember
that first litany,
Lamb of God,
to press my fist into my chest,
then make the casual sweeping sign
of the cross.
And the low sorrowing voice of the priest
did make me remember the death
that occurred every Sunday.

But kneeling alongside an elderly woman
I knew the best part of myself
wanted to be part of her,
part of the women
who lean together on street corners
and stand shading their eyes in doorways
and outlive their husbands.
And I remembered the last time
I'd been in a church

was the month my grandfather and a cousin
had died within weeks of each other.

I cried then
because no one had died before
or the words the priest said
weren't enough to make up for
a small child's life, even an old man's.
The only eloquence I remember
was my mother pressing a rose from his coffin
into my hand.

Reconciling

In grief
the body and spirit
wander side by side
each aware of the other's lonely presence,
door after door opening
through the balance of love
that threshold
where you, grieving now,
once said *here lies with there.*

From here
we are children again
asking for what they could never give us,
as if our voices
calling *mother, father*
from this distance
could name the first love we lost,
the loss that loss brings back.

But just as holding each other
the solid weight of our bodies
asks us to remember something more
than our sex,
just as the fir trees
outside my window hold their drifting shapes
in a sudden wind
swaying over me
as a parent comforting a child might,
being beyond being
there is some larger love.

It's when driving
through a deserted inner city
on a Sunday morning
I am driving there toward them,
wanting nothing more

than to stand in the kitchen doorway
of that windowless interior
its scraps of drawings, the soda bottles
on the cracked tiles of the counter.

There all we know
is how we love,
each life lived twice in parent and child—
they named us
for awhile called us hope
and we call back to them.

The Border

To possess something or someone, we must not surrender ourselves to it completely or lose our heads; in short we must remain superior to it. . . . Those who invented the love of God were pretty shrewd; there is nothing else we can possess and enjoy at the same time.—Cesare Pavese

i.

A woman sings in the next room
and unseen
leads the way into my dream,
or a friend's letter
its story of one day last autumn
lies waiting on a table
in another country:
at home it was already raining
they were hunting for mushrooms in the woods,
there the rain
drowned out the church bells,
the cries of birds. And
now in neither place
I remember the phone ringing at dusk
with news of your grandmother's death,
a woman I had never met,
how I held you
in that room
watery with twilight,
holding a man mourning
a woman who had held him.

ii.

I'm driving the long corridor of sound
on the interstate
until movement resembles no movement,
until the driver of the car next to me

signals *pull over*
and in the moment he pauses I am gone.

> *The vegetable hawker*
> *is ringing his bell, tomatoes*
> *and green beans heaped in the bed of his truck.*
> *He stops by the curb.*
> *"Can you tell time yet?"*
> *And the afternoon ends again,*
> *the shoe store, the bakery*
> *closing on each routine.*

I drove right by Connie and Rob's
in my old neighborhood.
I didn't want to know if she had
retired from factory work,
if he had stopped lifting new magazines
into the racks
and retiring last week's news.
The billboards
from the airport hotels towered
over the tract,
trees flattened under the glaring sky.
Even the market was gone
replaced by a square block of *light industry.*

Downtown
I made the same turn on Toluca
where First Street veers away from the bridge,
the bridge where the police shot
the deaf boy in the fog,
where somewhere in memory each aunt
picks up the telephone
and in a halo of lamplight worries
my deaf grandfather won't make it home.
But the street

where my mother and her mother grew up
is rubble.
The neighborhoods to the west
have changed from
Vietnamese to Nicaraguan to Salvadoran
in only five or six years.

I took my friend to the border.

"South of the City of Angels
lives my Aunt Juana,"
my grandmother used to say.
Her Anglo father kept their language
away from his children.
It was lost three generations back.

We want to make something beautiful
but we come to a border.

We *fuck up.*

The gaps in our language are as real
as the way we step out of it
into the world.

iii.

When you were in Mexico
you didn't know where you were going
or why. But the telegram
was phoned in, never delivered.
I heard the operator's voice:
"I am in Mérida.
I don't know where I am going or why."
And then you were gone—
unreachable—
yet like the ebb of a dream,

like the months the death of a woman,
a neighbor,
who mothered me
has stayed with me.

I've wanted a way to name that mourning,
the walk from a phone booth into the January fog
past the vendors selling oranges
on the Rialto Bridge
still hearing my mother's words:
"She's dead. She died on Thursday."
The news coming to me across distance
when I could have gone on without knowing.

> *Here are the candlesticks*
> *made of flowers and birds,*
> *hoops of the earrings, dahlias*
> *bobbing against a wall fluid in memory.*

And now I see
it is in the way we've called each other sister,
in the words we use for family,
that even then
not there,
where her life had been
where her burial would be,
her life was everywhere
part of every thing
that, like a landscape
where the clouds lie flat and low
mirroring the hills
until clouds and hills merge,
her death had turned her into the world.
She has never disappeared from my sight.

iv.

Over my desk
is a small photograph of my father
blasting the earth with a jackhammer.
Shirtless and strong, a straw hat circling his head,
his muscled body bowing to the pull of the hammer
was a perfect symbol of the CCCs, the thirties.
During the war the shrapnel
would lodge in his hands and his legs.
In the fifties his body bloated with alcohol,
the tiny pieces of metal drifting
in a sea of flesh and veins.

v.

Man is like a thing of nought: his time passeth away like a shadow.
                                    —*from* Holy Dying *by Jeremy Taylor*

I play with the baby—
ask if she remembers the line
of fur her mother described
that ran across her forehead,
tell her the story of the sperm.
I'm pretty funny today.
She's already forgotten who I am.

On a speaking tour of the Northwest
a South African woman,
exiled to Botswana since 1962,
began her talk by saying
"Let me tell you about the children
in my country . . ."

I remember how a friend from El Salvador
sat talking, fingering the small hole

59

the size of a bullet at the knee of his son's pants.
In El Paso, Texas, this morning
a woman was deported, the plane
crossing the border in heavy rains
back to El Salvador.

Each night we sit around this table in America,
two stones, the wooden bowl
at its center. When
you were gone
the bowl held plums and we wrote
our words addressed to wherever you were
though the letters would never reach you
come home.

The history of each of us
is a call across distance
trying to name so many wounds
until finally we call death
an absence
when nothing can name the absent
their constant falling from this world.

August 1983—August 1985

A JOURNEY

The Drunkard: Our Song

You were a boy
climbing the stairs of a house
just off Main Street, no light
the stairs twisting
and you reached for the railing.
When you opened the door at the top
the air was full of your parents' cries.
Your hand raised as if to hold back
your mother's body from falling,
the noise that drifted up from the street,
the flesh wounding flesh.

And something else,
something you began to understand even then.
No one would turn to you.
No one would hold you.
So you wrapped yourself in the threads of song
you pulled from your throat,
your eyes flecked with motion,
frozen with memory's simple photographs—
Years later your mother in that room
unable to move as she slowly died of a stroke,
growing larger and larger
until she seemed an island
filling your ocean of grief.

One August I found,
hidden in a trunk in the garage,
a photograph of her on her bier—
massive grandmother
floating in a sea of lilies, yet
a weight in my hands in that heat.

Through the windowscreen
you wouldn't answer my call;
two shifts and a fifth of Jim Beam a day

and you slept. Some nights
I watched the same struggles:
the invitations to mother to crack your head
with a glass, to my brother to push all of your
soft, sad weight to the floor. Your grief
was so large my childhood was hazy with it,
as if I struggled like a swimmer
up toward the surface of light.

Now I have sat in the woods
until the owl's wings slapped over me,
lain with the bat winging through the room
trying to remember the reason for sadness.
Until I understand that even grown
you and I were still children
who stood watching,
humming a song
that froze the world in the shape of our own grief
only as large as your mother,
island, or cloud. Or you,
my father, sprawled
in your silence, not even
a sheet to cover that nakedness.

Hospital

Lifting her arm
she pulls her hand toward her face.
I can see the loose flesh of her underarm,
the sleeve of her dress
bunching around her shoulder,
the weight of her arm pulling the children
on bikes down the street toward her.

I am traveling toward dusk,
traveling toward the arms of dusk.
The branch tips are reddening,
it is raining and a warm wind blowing
the hand that held me down rising—
a woman stands in a doorway
calling her children home;
they can see her cotton wash dress billowing.
No, she is in the next bed;
she is here with us seeing them.

Like a train whistle that begins as a calling,
and arcing across a plain that is our life
returns as an echo of its own calling,
her memory has no boundary.
Now I hear her saying,
You can do anything to me.
Her first name is the same as mine;
she is as old as my mother.
You can do anything;
my body is beyond anything you can do.

She was scared, no makeup,
just out of surgery. She wanted
something to be reasonable. For once
she wanted something to be reasonable,

wanted him to see
he shouldn't have taken me out of school
for the long trip downtown at midday.
You shouldn't have brought her.
I looked at the next bed,
a woman was swinging her legs over the side,
her hospital gown pulling apart to reveal
the long dignified curve of her spine.

A Ferry Crossing

In the five or ten minutes
it takes dusk to settle into evening
the ferry is crossing
from one orchard to the other.

I'm tired
as the cables overhead
drag the awkward barge
through the current.
And here
almost at water level
it's as if I'm part of the river
just as dreaming
I've thought we are one with our dreams.

But dreaming
I glimpse the ruby throat
of a hummingbird by the woodbox,
or another bird
mourning its mate
its mouth suddenly opening
to swallow the dead,
and here on the river
the current beneath me
is like all that's unspoken,
though every denial will say it exists,
when we want what another can't give.

It is Sunday night
and I am trying to find something in myself.
It's in the orchard
the years it took the farmer to grow
the budding rows,
or the patience of the ferry man,
how he loves the wide barge
and the slow pride of its crossing.

A Healing Song

—for Bahati Ansari

The making of tea
steam battering the windows
in preparation for a departure,
and in the next room
one bathed the other
rubbing her with alcohol and powder
massaging her to sleep,
not the emptiness of travel
but the bridge of hands
that led her on.

It has been a year
since I broke into my life. Some days
wanting movement
or the larger change,
I forget
to love the glimpsed underside of wings,
white bellies and orange collars
of the juvenile robins
skimming wet leaves for insects,
to be amazed that through this window
I should see them.

Crossing the dunes at the end of summer,
up through the grasses to the sea,
my friend ran past me to the waves
then turned and fell into my arms
laughing then crying
then turning to walk down the beach.

I have mourned the past
its elegies, its endings,
but the future,
like the sea we walked against
earth unraveling at its edge,

68

has begun to open
on its terrifying form
and it comes in bending and preparation
in cleansing and small change
in every detail that mocks emptiness.

Atlas

The huge pages of an atlas
lay open on a table,
as if the world had spread its secrets
benign and tactile
in the sensuous blues of oceans
under lamplight.

At dinner I listened
to the others talking. And listening, knowing
that in the years they had worked
and traveled I had remained here,
deep in the grief that clouded everything,
that uneasy plane
came back.

It's like watching someone die.
It's like seeing your own death very near you.

There, at the table,
it was close to me again,
unresolved,
the years that have to die before us
or they become our own death,
have to die before they have a chance
to make us love them, listen
to what they have to say,
old anger, for parents, lost love, loss.

But now,
one sister carrying the other's voice,
or a friend saying *I'll show you ironweed*
car hurtling past something I have seen before,
now there is *knowing*
and that becomes its own departure:

All night I've dreamt,
rain drumming the roof,

of the waves that reach across a road,
but we are safe,
all of us in dream's embrace,
the skin that does cloak bone, blood,
dried petals under glass.

We move quickly now.
We must move quicker than our own despair.

Salem: Two Windows

I'm sitting at a friend's table
watching a young woman
hold on to the railing
as she climbs the front steps to her house.
Her small daughter follows behind
carrying a bag of groceries too big for her.
Now the woman turns,
many months pregnant,
and closes the door
leaving me to think about silence,
the line of tension pulling at me,
its denial.

Driving here
I wanted to name everything
as if naming would say it was not part of me—
the giant paper mill
and its constant yellow flame,
the smell of pulp that spills
over the collars of children in schools
called Sunrise and Mountain View,
Spring blurred by mud and sleet
in the milltowns that I passed.

I teach. I tell the kids
don't censor, let the self out you didn't
know you had. There's a boy in class
who remembers how light flickers through trees
when he stands knee deep in stream water fishing,
who says *I don't know if you'll understand*
but there are voices coming through me;
and born in 1968,
a child who listened around the kitchen table,

he speaks his uncle's tongues
on some airstrip in Vietnam.

The girl is on the street again tossing a ball—
it lands in her hands,
that's the simple law of gravity.
To my right a window facing a wall of bricks,
winter sunlight staining the glass
though I can't see its source,
and the bare branches of a bush
ready to blossom.

Reading Grimm's Fairy Tales

I had forgotten the bird
hunger or happiness in its call
blossoming against the clear sky,
the cat,
balanced on hind legs, mannerly,
even as its claws sunk into the plumage
of the bird's curved chest,
or what I learned alone each night,
bird alighting on the blade of a knife
hidden in the ivy
and suffering a transformation
that made its last cry human.

By day the cat tossed a sparrow,
bit the mouse cleanly in half.
I saw my brother
hosing maggots from a garbage can.
I saw blood flecked with human hair
pooled next to a white enamel pan
on the kitchen floor:
viscous,
holding to its own circle
I saw it held everything.

I wanted the iridescence of their wings,
their generous hearts.
I found the skull of a bird
and buried it,
clean whistle that sights the world,
in a wooden box.

What I can't stand even now,
summer, birds drifting from branch to branch,
is that fluttering,
as if in their wings
were their caged hearts
waiting for the cry we give them,
waiting to alight on death.

Let Go

—for Diane Reed

It is summer
necessary in its fragmentation,
dogs bark,
broken glass and weeds line the road,
the birds are thick in the woods this morning.
There is no shape
to the sliding undercurrent
of the domed butte,
the volcano.

❋

The child at the beginning of the scream
learns not to scream;
she learns nothing is beautiful
but the deepest lie coiling within her
makes it beautiful—
this is the beginning of corruption,
of what eats the soul,
the child poised in its doorway
looking for some way to sing,
to believe in the singing.

❋

Wings beat overhead,
a small bird has landed on the arm of the chair
eyes pulsing, breathing hard.
No, it does not know I am here.
At the same moment the cat and I
see the chipmunk.

I am not the farthest point from anywhere
I have ever been.
The palm trees are gone,
as are the new books, the new words.
Time is not marked by wandering over distance
or blessed by a bottle of beer

or a loaf of bread laced with olives.

❋

The scream is real,
twisting through the clouded eye,
the convolute vision,
it has possibility—
it believes in its own way. No, I believe
it must find its way through the summer,
through the terror of sunlight,
this landscape:
the boy who stands urinating under the bridge
cars crossing above him like dry beetles.

❋

What did I like?

The place where the body ceased to bear the soul,
where the two came together
acting as one.
There the landscape welcomed me,
the moon rose from behind a hilltop
and resting there
for a moment in that surreal past
I could touch it.
I swear I ran toward it—
we all did.

❋

Where was the place I labored,
what has said this was important,
what has said it was not?

Now to see the child
is to understand she will never be found,
this is my shape
beaded with water, with light.

A Journey

I am walking
and I think: it's a cold wind
blowing through my soul,
a little blade that turns.

But this time it's different.
I don't picture the soul the way I did
years ago, leaving the body
for the trees
when the trees were women swaying,
bending to cradle me.

This time the soul and the body
are all mixed up: I walk
through a marketplace where vendors sell
olives, saffron, honey, and thyme.
Now I part clouds like curtains, light
when there is light, shifting
in and out behind them.

And then, sometimes,
there is nothing. It is enormous
this place where I am falling through myself.
That's when the wind comes,
blowing down streets open and raw.
There, where there might have been a child,
are the squat stucco houses,
the voices lifting and pulling,
rending the air
after each day of work.

Now everywhere I look there are children.
Men and women carrying children
brush against me, and someone
is playing the saxophone.
The player is sad.
I can hear the sad notes

but the player plays right through the sadness.
The sadness becomes something.

I don't know, maybe I thought I was smart,
or right,
yes, right and the rightness filled me up
with words that were certain as stone
that made me sink
so I didn't feel this wind.

Vision

—to Brigit Kelly

I was lonely on an empty road
but around the next turn—
flares, ambulance, and gray police cars,
men huddling against the cold
holding coffee, cigarettes
that gave off earthly clouds of steam,
and in a muddy field others kneeling—
as if mourners around a grave
who try to hold the spirit's place.

Someone had run from the house.
Someone had died.
Someone was running still.

I don't know what holds us here.

Sometimes I choose an icon
that won't look like a god,
white bone opening on the bluest sky, or
baskets of lobelia, geraniums
sun-struck and blossoming against the wind.
Once I dreamt square blocks of sandstone.
I believed I could make the world simple with stone,
with walls
that bloomed against the sea,
seawall, waves washing and eroding all in good time,
with days that began walking down one cobbled street
with bread, the baker
all sustaining us.

But if the bread goes bad,
what is the source?
It is the grain, it is the soil we touch.
We touch the world,
why should we think it is not in us?

The Garden

Often I dream the plot of earth
in the center of the yard
behind the house where I grew up.
There, I dream a garden. This year,
I think, in this place
where nothing is ever finished,
in this place that I fled
because I did not want them to touch me
and so have wanted no one
to touch me, in this place
I have come back to plant a garden.

And in my dreams
each year the garden fails
each year it is an afterthought,
something I begin and cannot finish.
One year I plant tomatoes
and forget to water them—
even when I tell myself to remember
I forget. And the next year
there is too much rain
so the squash grow bloated and soft;
they grow so large that the tip of my shoe
nudging one splits its flesh,
just as yesterday I pushed
at what I thought was a green bead
and crushed a shimmering bug
for no other reason than
I was large and stupid and human.

There, in the center of the yard,
with the prop planes flying so low
I can read the numbers on their wings
and the jets lowering their bellies

to land only a mile away
—the incredible blast of their engines
drowning out the voice of anything
on the ground—
there, with the smell of the Frito factory,
with the pink oleanders and their poisonous leaves
and the stunted avocado tree,
there, with the dog whose ribs show
because she cannot stop running,
snapping at the noise
in the air we can't breathe.

There I am
standing in the yard
thinking we should have had a garden.
There was so much sun,
things would have been different
if there had been something to tend,
or the sense of a season
in which we could tend it.

We Never Knew You

—to the memory of my grandmother, Helen Greeley, 1898–1986

Late February
bougainvillaea, orange trees beginning to blossom,
eucalyptus rustling and scraping overhead
all claim their presence
in the stagnant air
and you are dead.
And I believe the body houses pain,
I see that now, I believe the body houses pain
until it is ready to give it up
and I don't know why it took so long.

As if I'd never left,
part of them as they are part of me,
the room is filled with aunts, uncles, cousins,
even my own parents;
roast in the oven, tequila
and Johnny Walker on the table top
we mourn. Your children
are telling stories about you in a good year,
the good year meant to hold you here among us:
*Mama always knew when someone was coming
she'd start to bake the bread.*
Not, Mama tried to burn the house down
and take him with it, or
after he handcuffed her to the table
Mama took a knife up in revenge.
It took me years to find those things out,
as if in their silence
they meant to blame you.

But maybe there was something else.
Maybe there was flight.
Maybe you fled long ago.

Let's say the body is no house, no rack of pain.
Let's say at the beginning of the Depression

a woman goes to the hospital to give birth
to her seventh child.
But something happens
she doesn't come home for six years.
And she's not in the ward of the state hospital—
shock therapy jolting
the sad designation of flesh,
begging to come home
though her husband will not sign the release—
she's not there at all.

No one knows where she went.

And one day when she comes home
and her oldest girls are women
and she doesn't know the youngest child
and her husband's live-in friend
has left only the day before,
on that day everyone tries to pretend
she has never been away.

And you live the years silent and drugged
with the secret of where you have been.
Until something, a grown son dying,
or a friend's husband taking a shotgun
to a son-in-law for beating a daughter,
any of the daily wars
among the larger wars of those years—
breaks through
and then you are gone,
you are flying again.

Now, little grandmother,
it is finally over. And I believe in endings
in the symmetry you never had in life,
so I'm trying to see a woman

bending among clay pots in that dusty garden,
to see birds, bread, or flowers,
to see you as photos show you one of those good years—
still beautiful
smiling into the face of yet another grandchild—
but I can't.

At the cemetery entrance in East L.A.
we buy you irises,
armloads of yellow gladiolus
and bury you alongside the old man,
dead in the time of another war,
your graves among the graves
of nineteen- and twenty-year-olds
killed in Vietnam.
Your family gathered
we give you back to them
their beautiful names,
Miguel and Jesús and Ramón,
your own name lost at birth
your own war over,
tombstone laid to the side
engraved with his LAPD badge and your rosary,
our heads bowed in all that we are,
our casual sweetness, our casual hatreds,
we thank you for our lives.

Desire in America

Like the humming of insects
through the last days of summer, or
the juice of a peach spilling into the dust,
like something glimpsed
in the pink sheen of the glass buildings
that for a moment mirror sunset,
we pursue it
thinking we love
what won't be contained,
as if it were something
outside of ourselves.

We pursue it
until every sensation of dailiness,
the boy tending a garden, plates
slapping the table, the child
just learning to say *No,*
is dulled, until
what we want
turns as bitterly tangible
as a seed that splits in our mouths.

Then,
like that boy's death,
his body found
in a shallow grave by the neighbors
saying *This boy wasn't swearing.*
This boy was fishing
and tending tomatoes all summer,
our loss is unrealized
as we swallow each other,
as we allow one country to swallow another,
in the hand-to-hand combat of each death.

When all along
something constant

blurred and unfocused, the suffusion
of flat prairie or even line of the sea,
nights we lay in each other's arms
simple and peaceful
our faces alive beyond what we had known
to call desire,
might have existed,
something labored and loved
the way the boy loved the garden,
the way we might have loved the boy
if we had loved something in ourselves
that could love him.

About the Author

Maxine Scates was born in Los Angeles, California, in 1949. She studied English Literature at California State University, Northridge, where she earned a B.A., and writing at the University of Oregon, where she received her M.F.A. In 1988 she received an Ed. M. in Adult Education (Literacy, Developmental Writing, English as a Second Language) from Oregon State University. From 1981 to 1985 she was poetry editor of *Northwest Review*. She lives in Eugene, Oregon.

PITT POETRY SERIES

Ed Ochester, General Editor

Dannie Abse, *Collected Poems*
Claribel Alegría, *Flowers from the Volcano*
Claribel Alegría, *Woman of the River*
Maggie Anderson, *Cold Comfort*
Michael Benedikt, *The Badminton at Great Barrington; Or, Gustave Mahler
   & the Chattanooga Choo-Choo*
Michael Burkard, *Ruby for Grief*
Siv Cedering, *Letters from the Floating World*
Lorna Dee Cervantes, *Emplumada*
Robert Coles, *A Festering Sweetness: Poems of American People*
Kate Daniels, *The Niobe Poems*
Kate Daniels, *The White Wave*
Toi Derricotte, *Captivity*
Norman Dubie, *Alehouse Sonnets*
Stuart Dybek, *Brass Knuckles*
Odysseus Elytis, *The Axion Esti*
Jane Flanders, *Timepiece*
Gary Gildner, *Blue Like the Heavens: New & Selected Poems*
Bruce Guernsey, *January Thaw*
Barbara Helfgott Hyett, *In Evidence: Poems of the Liberation of Nazi
   Concentration Camps*
Milne Holton and Paul Vangelisti, eds., *The New Polish Poetry: A Bilingual
   Collection*
David Huddle, *Paper Boy*
Phyllis Janowitz, *Temporary Dwellings*
Lawrence Joseph, *Curriculum Vitae*
Lawrence Joseph, *Shouting at No One*
Etheridge Knight, *The Essential Etheridge Knight*
Bill Knott, *Poems: 1963–1988*
Ted Kooser, *One World at a Time*
Ted Kooser, *Sure Signs: New and Selected Poems*
Larry Levis, *Winter Stars*
Larry Levis, *Wrecking Crew*
Robert Louthan, *Living in Code*
Tom Lowenstein, tr., *Eskimo Poems from Canada and Greenland*
Irene McKinney, *Six O'Clock Mine Report*